THE NATIONAL TRUST

D0537421

Investigating CHILDHOOD in Tudor and Victorian Times

By Laura Wilson

Illustrated by Peter Stevenson

CONTENTS

Who were the Tudors?

The Tudor era was a period that lasted 118 years in the fifteenth and sixteenth centuries. It was called 'Tudor' because the kings and queens who ruled England and Wales during that time were descended from a Welshman, Owen Tudor.

The struggle for power

The first Tudor king was Henry VII. He gained the throne in 1485 after a civil war in which the two most powerful families in England, the houses of York and Lancaster, fought each other. Henry Tudor, who was a Lancastrian, won. He united the two houses by marrying Elizabeth of York in 1486.

The next king was Henry VIII who is famous for having six wives. He came to the throne in 1509. When he died in 1547, his son *(below)* was crowned Edward VI.

> After the wars, the Yorkist symbol, a white rose, was merged with the red rose of Lancaster to make the two-coloured Tudor rose.

Edward was only nine when he became king, and did not live long. In 1553 he was succeeded by his half-sister, Mary. She died five years later and their half-sister, Elizabeth I became queen. None of them had children so the Tudor dynasty ended with Elizabeth in 1603.

The Tudor period was a dramatic time. England and Wales stopped being Catholic when Henry VIII split from the Church of Rome after divorcing his first wife. Then, under Edward, Mary and Elizabeth, the country went from Protestant to Catholic and back again, as each monarch imposed his or her religion. Priests were forced into hiding.

Tudor symbols on the painted ceiling in the chapel of Ightham Mote, Kent

Short lives

Tudors who survived babyhood could only expect to live until around the age of 40. The average height of a Tudor man was 1.71m, and a Tudor woman, 1.57m. Henry VIII, at 1.85m, was very tall.

Travelling on foot

Most people had only one method of transport – their feet. The rich travelled on horseback or in carriages, which were few and far between, and very bumpy and uncomfortable. People rarely travelled outside their own parish, and even Queen Elizabeth did not visit many parts of her kingdom.

The trouble with Mary

Scotland was a separate kingdom, although there were links between the royal families – Henry VIII's sister Margaret was married to James IV of Scotland.

This link caused trouble later. Many people wanted Margaret's granddaughter, Mary, Queen of Scots, to be queen of England instead of her cousin Elizabeth.

When Mary was forced to flee to England after a rebellion in Scotland, Elizabeth kept her a virtual prisoner in various great houses.

Mary, Queen of Scots spent some of her boring captivity doing embroidery. If you visit Oxburgh Hall in Norfolk, or Hardwick Hall in Derbyshire (where this portrait hangs), you can see her work.

From wars to watches

There were rebellions and wars, including attempts by Spain to invade England.

Voyages of exploration resulted in the first visit of British people to America. There were discoveries under the Tudors, such as the potato and the tobacco plant, and inventions, including the pocket watch and the pencil.

Babies galore

At the start of the Tudor era, the population of the kingdom was around 2.6 million. By 1600, it had grown to 4 million. Ninety per cent of these people lived and worked in the countryside. The population of London was around 50,000 in 1485 but had grown to over 200,000 by 1603.

3

And who were the Victorians?

Queen Victoria is Britain's longest reigning monarch. When she came to the throne, aged eighteen, in 1837, the country was far more like Tudor England than modern Britain. By the time she died 64 years later, in 1901, her kingdom had changed beyond recognition, with a network of railways, a postal service, and many houses having electricity and mains water. The Victorians invented much of what we take for granted today, such as anaesthetics, the telephone and the camera.

The Industrial Revolution

A huge change came about during the eighteenth and nineteenth centuries as people learnt more about science and invented machines. These could mass-produce everything from water pipes to pots and pans. Things could be cheaper than ever before.

The wonder of electricity: at Cragside, Northumberland in the 1880s

Factory workers

New farming machinery meant that there was less work in the countryside, so many families moved into the rapidly growing towns to get jobs in the new factories. This meant that by 1851 more people in England lived in the towns than in the countryside.

Children as well as adults joined the workforce. Called the 'workshop of the world', Britain became both the greatest trading nation and the richest country.

Shrink to fit

The Victorians were shorter than their Tudor ancestors – the average man was 1.66m and the average woman, 1.56m. At 1.52m, Queen Victoria was on the short side. The drop in height may have been caused by the poor diet and living conditions in cities.

In the 1880s, a town worker had a life expectancy of only 30 years, while a country worker might expect to live for 52 years.

New transport for a works outing to Teignmouth, Devon in 1854

Improvements everywhere?

The spread of the railways across the country made it easier for people to travel. As the nineteenth century progressed, they also benefited from improved schools, advances in medicine and, for some, better working conditions.

A population explosion

In 1838, a year after Queen Victoria came to the throne, the population of the country was 15.3 million. By 1901, it was up to 32.6 million. At the beginning of the Victorian era, 38 per cent of the population lived in towns. By 1901, this was 77 per cent. Between 1851 and 1911, London grew from a city of 2.3 million inhabitants to one of 7.1 million.

Expanding the empire

Although Victoria's reign was a peaceful time for people living in Britain (which by this time included Scotland and all of Ireland as well as England and Wales), the British army fought many wars in foreign countries.

The British Empire included India, Egypt and other parts of Africa, as well as Australia, New Zealand and Canada. By 1901, the empire was so large that it was said that 'the sun never set' on it because it was always daytime somewhere.

The Tudor Royal Family

There were five Tudor monarchs altogether. Only one, Edward VI, the son of Henry VIII's third wife, was destined from birth to be crowned.

Henry VII
r. 1485-1509
m. Elizabeth of York

Arthur
(died 1502)
m. Catherine of Aragon

Henry VIII
r. 1509-1547

Margaret

Mary

m. Catherine of Aragon

m. Anne Boleyn

m. Jane Seymour

Mary I
r. 1553-58
m. Philip II of Spain

Elizabeth I
r. 1558-1603

Edward VI
r. 1547-53

Henry and his wives

Henry VIII inherited his brother Arthur's Spanish wife, Catherine of Aragon – the first of his six wives. Henry wanted a son and was disappointed when Catherine gave birth to a baby girl, Mary. He divorced his wife when Mary was in her mid-teens and married Anne Boleyn. She also failed to produce the son that Henry hoped for and was executed.

His third wife was Jane Seymour, followed by Anne of Cleves, Catherine Howard and, last of all, Catherine Parr.

A son and heir

As Mary was Catholic she did not recognise her father's divorce but he declared her illegitimate and when Anne Boleyn gave birth to a baby girl, Elizabeth, he made Mary wait on her half-sister.

When Elizabeth was nearly three years old her father married Jane Seymour who, at last, produced a son, Edward. It was now Elizabeth's turn to be deprived of the title of princess.

A portrait of Henry VIII by Holbein

NTPL / JOHN HAMMOND

Strange childhoods

Tudor noblemen and women did not spend a great deal of time with their children. Mary, Elizabeth and Edward grew up in separate houses, with their own servants and tutors. Henry did not often visit his daughters, but sent courtiers to make sure that they were well.

From court to the Tower

Elizabeth was ignored by Henry's fourth and fifth wives but, along with Mary and Edward, found a mother figure in Henry's last wife, Catherine Parr. She brought the children to court to live together at last. By this time Elizabeth, aged ten, probably had very little memory of her own mother, Anne Boleyn, because nobody ever mentioned her name.

Not surprisingly, Mary and Elizabeth (who was brought up as a Protestant) did not get on well, so when Mary became queen, she had Elizabeth imprisoned in the Tower of London.

Favourite stepmothers

Both Mary and Elizabeth had a series of stepmothers as their father kept remarrying.

Mary didn't get on with Elizabeth's mother, Anne Boleyn, but Edward's mother, Jane Seymour, was very kind to her. She begged Henry to allow Mary to return to court. He agreed, and even let Mary have her title back. When Jane Seymour died, Mary was said to be 'crazed [mad] with sorrow'.

Mary liked Henry's fourth wife, Anne of Cleves, but not his fifth, Katherine Howard, who was five years younger than she was.

NTPL / RICHARD PINK

A portrait of Elizabeth I, which shows that she inherited Henry VIII's love of fine clothes

The Victorian Royal Family

Queen Victoria was born on 24 May 1819 at Kensington Palace. She was christened Alexandrina Victoria, and as a little girl was known as 'Drina'. Her father, Edward, Duke of Kent, was the fourth son of George III. Her mother was a German princess, Victoria of Saxe-Coburg-Saalfeld.

Victoria's father died when she was only eight months old. When she was six, parliament realised that Victoria would become queen because George IV and William IV, her uncles, had no surviving legitimate heirs.

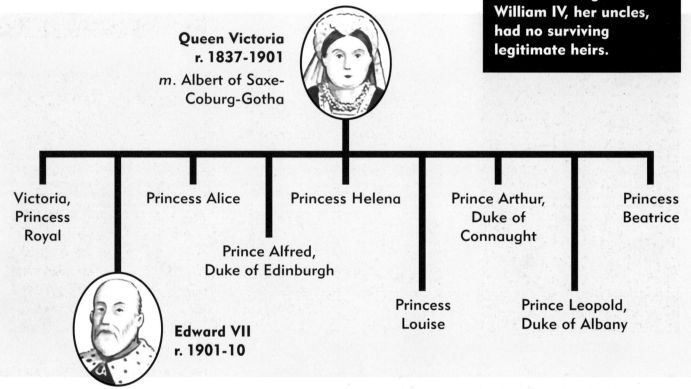

Queen Victoria
r. 1837-1901
m. Albert of Saxe-Coburg-Gotha

Victoria, Princess Royal

Princess Alice

Prince Alfred, Duke of Edinburgh

Edward VII
r. 1901-10

Princess Helena

Princess Louise

Prince Arthur, Duke of Connaught

Prince Leopold, Duke of Albany

Princess Beatrice

An only child

Victoria and her mother lived simply in a suite of rooms at Kensington Palace in London. As an adult, she was to describe her childhood as a lonely time.

She had few friends of her own age and felt 'crushed and kept under and hardly dared say a word'.

Perhaps it was her mother who did the 'crushing', because young Victoria seems to have preferred her governess, Louise Lehzen. The Duchess often quarrelled with members of the royal household. This must have been unpleasant for Victoria, who tended to lose her temper and then burst into tears at moments of stress.

The teenage queen

Many people felt sorry for Victoria, because she had to take on such a great responsibility so young. She became queen when she was only eighteen.

Moving into Buckingham Palace, Victoria was afraid that her mother would interfere in royal affairs, so banished her to the suite of rooms furthest from her own. After her coronation in 1838, Thomas Carlyle wrote:

'Poor little Queen! She is at an age at which a girl can hardly be trusted to choose a bonnet for herself; yet a task is laid on her from which an archangel might shrink.'

Queen Victoria with her mother

COURTAULD INSTITUTE OF ART

Family life

In 1840 Victoria married her cousin, Prince Albert of Saxe-Coburg-Gotha. They had nine children but she did not in fact like babies. She wrote:

'...an ugly baby is a very nasty object, and the prettiest is frightful when undressed'.

A Prime Minister comes to tea

The young queen had lots of help from Lord Melbourne, her first Prime Minister. As well as explaining political affairs to her, he also helped her with spelling and played with her beloved spaniel, Dash. She wrote in her diary:

'We put him [Dash] on the table, and he was very much petted and patted by Lord M... We gave him tea, and Lord M. said "I wonder if lapping is a pleasant sensation," for it was a thing we never had felt.'

Escape to the Isle of Wight

Victoria spent more time with her children than many parents at that time. 'I quite admit the comfort and blessing of good and amiable children,' she wrote, 'though they are also an awful plague and anxiety'. She complained that the nurseries at Buckingham Palace were so far away from her own apartments that she had to walk 'literally a mile' to see them.

The Queen and Prince Albert made a wonderful home for their family at Osborne House on the Isle of Wight. Albert had a play-house built where the children cooked in a miniature kitchen *(right)*. He encouraged them to start a museum, and people all over the empire sent curiosities for them to label and put in glass cases. They also had their own gardens, and the boys had a child-sized fort for playing soldiers.

© ENGLISH HERITAGE PHOTO LIBRARY

Swiss Cottage, at Osborne House, where the royal children played

Victorian attitudes to children

The Victorians thought that family life was very important. They had an idealised picture of the perfect family, based on the idea of 'Home, Sweet Home' – the father was in charge, the mother an 'angel in the house', and quiet, well-behaved children enjoyed being good.

A sculpture at Wallington in Northumberland showing 'ideal' Victorian motherhood

NTPL

Let children that would
fear the Lord
Hear what their teachers
say:
With reverence meet
their parent's word
And with delight obey.

A verse from *Divine and Moral Songs for Children* by Isaac Watts

All sorts of families

Of course, the truth was rather different from the ideal. There were many loving, happy families, but there were also plenty of miserable ones.

Although divorce was possible – if difficult – it was expensive and not socially acceptable. So unhappy couples usually could not separate, but had to make the best of it.

Ideal homes?

Victorians with money took great pride in their homes, cramming every corner with furniture, pictures and ornaments. However, many poor children grew up in homes almost empty of belongings. Some, like the orphans found by Dr Barnardo on the streets of London in 1866, had no homes at all.

Little angels

The Victorians had a very different attitude from the Tudors: they believed children were innocent, not sinful, and sometimes tried to make childhood last as long as possible.

Although the Victorians thought of childhood as separate from adulthood, there was no recognised 'in-between' stage, like being a teenager today. The point at which children became adults depended on whether they were boys or girls, rich or poor – it might be putting your hair up for a wealthy girl, or bringing home your first day's pay for a chimney boy.

'Read the instructions'

There were many books giving parents advice about how to bring up their children but they were aimed at the educated parent, not at the poor.

The odd slap

The Victorians shared with the Tudors the belief that beating children was a good way to make them behave. Even Queen Victoria, whose first child was born in 1840, said that it was necessary to give the 'the odd slap' from time to time.

Underfed and overworked

Some children grew up weak and unhealthy from lack of good food, and were made to work long hours. Some were treated unkindly by their parents. The government was reluctant to pass any laws to protect them.

The National Society for the Prevention of Cruelty to Children (NSPCC) was founded in 1884, some years after the Royal Society for the Prevention of Cruelty to Animals (RSPCA). Children were not fully protected from cruelty *by law* until 1908.

Ideas started to change by the end of the century. When the Norland Nursing School was founded in 1892 the nannies who trained there were told not to hit children because 'the Norland Institute does not recognise the necessity of whipping or slapping' – a very modern attitude.

NTPL

A portrait showing 'the father in charge' with his 'obedient' son

How Tudor children lived

There was a great contrast between the lives of children from different backgrounds. Children of the Tudor nobility lived in grand houses with servants and private tutors. Poor children started working young in order to help their parents in the fields or the family trade.

No room of their own

Tudor children, whether rich or poor, very rarely had their own special rooms, such as nurseries. Small houses or cottages were often crowded with several families living under the same roof.

Lady Anne Clifford, who came from a very wealthy family, wrote of her childhood in the 1590s:

'I used to go much to the Court and sometimes I did lie at my Aunt Warwick's chamber on a pallett [straw mattress]...'

NTPL / MIKE WILLIAMS

Hardwick Hall in Derbyshire, where rich and powerful Bess of Hardwick kept her granddaughter Arabella almost a prisoner

Arabella Stuart was still made to sleep in her grandmother's bedroom at the age of 27. Bess of Hardwick wrote:

'At such time as she shall take the air it shall be near the house and well attended on. She goeth not to anybody's house at all. I see her almost every hour of the day.'

Not surprisingly, Arabella grew from a pretty child into an awkward young woman. She wanted to escape, and told the chaplain that 'she thought of all means she could to get from home'.

Bess of Hardwick: from a modest childhood she grew to be very wealthy as Countess of Shrewsbury

Placing out

In a late fifteenth-century book, an Italian visitor to England describes the people as not having much love for their children:

'…having kept them at home till they arrive at the age of seven or nine years at the utmost, they put them out, both males and females, to hard service in the houses of other people… everyone, however rich he may be, sends away his children into the houses of others, whilst he, in return, receives those of strangers into his own'.

Bringing up Bess

Bess of Hardwick was herself 'placed out' as a child. In 1540, she was sent to Codnor Castle in Derbyshire, home of Sir John and Lady Zouche, as a 'gentlewoman' or upper servant. There she learnt the manners and skills she would need as she grew up. It was where she met Robert Barlow, who was to become the first of her four husbands.

Sharing out the load

Poor children were also sent to live with other families. It was a good way of sharing out labour – one family might have several strong daughters and sons to help in the house and the fields, while another family might have none. A boy might be sent to a craftsman as an apprentice, to learn a trade.

How Victorian children lived

Although Britain was very rich in the nineteenth century, the wealth was not shared equally. Many families were desperately poor. If they lost their jobs, there was no social security to help them, and they might end up in a workhouse. This was almost as bad as being in prison, because families would be split up and forced to work in return for a little food and a place to sleep.

NTPL / ANDREW BUTLER

The workhouse at Thurgaton, Nottinghamshire

The more the merrier?

Large families were very common. Queen Victoria and Prince Albert, for instance, had nine children. To poor people, this could be a terrible burden, because another child meant one more mouth to feed and yet more hardship.

'Seen but not heard'

Wealthy Victorians did not spend very much time with their children, as most were looked after by nannies. The children played and ate their meals in the nursery and only came downstairs to be presented to their mother and father before they went to bed.

The nursery wing at Lanhydrock in Cornwall is where the ten children of Lord and Lady Robartes grew up. The wing includes a day nursery, a night nursery (right) where the children slept, a schoolroom, a bedroom for the nanny, a scullery and a bathroom. It is all linked by staircases to the kitchen quarters and to the servants' bedrooms.

NTPL / ANDREAS VON EINSIEDEL

Nannies rule – OK?

Nannies were often the most important people in their charges' lives, as the children saw far more of them than they did of their parents. The nanny was always there to listen to their secrets, tell them stories and comfort them if they were unhappy.

A miserable time

Unfortunately, not all nannies were kind. The distinguished politician, Lord Curzon, wrote of his nanny, Miss Paraman:

'She... beat us with her brushes, tied us for long hours to chairs in uncomfortable positions with our hands holding a pole or a blackboard behind our backs, shut us up in darkness...'

Winston Churchill, the future Prime Minister, was lucky with the person chosen to be his nanny. After the death of Mrs Everest, he wrote:

'She had been my dearest... friend during the whole of the 20 years I had lived'.

Like some other children from wealthy families, Churchill remembered his mother as a distant, goddess-like being:

'She shone for me like the Evening Star. I loved her dearly – but at a distance.'

Other mothers

In poor families, where both parents had to go out to work, babies and young children were looked after by a grandmother, an older sister, or a neighbour, who might be paid a few pennies for keeping an eye on them.

'A typical "little mother" of the London doorstep... She is nursing a heavy baby who is perhaps a year old... But every other minute her attention is distracted by the conduct of a sister, aged four, and a brother, aged five...'

A description of an eight-year-old girl, from *How the Poor Live*, written in 1883

Nurseries to visit:

● Arlington Court, Devon
● Calke Abbey, Derbyshire
● Lanhydrock, Cornwall
● Wightwick Manor, West Midlands

Tudor babies

Whether you were rich or poor, having a baby in the sixteenth century was a dangerous business. Many women, including Henry VIII's third queen, Jane Seymour, died in childbirth. Being a baby was dangerous, too. Many infants died before their first birthday.

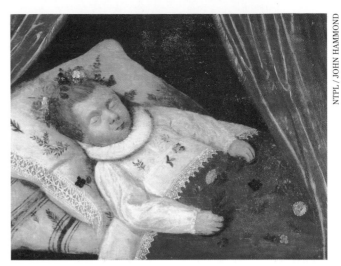

Portrait of a dead child, 1620, at Oxburgh Hall, Norfolk

The sad experience of Lady Anne Clifford was not an unusual one:

'I had by him [her first husband, Richard Sackville] five children, viz. three sons and two daughters. The three sons all dyed young …but my first child the Lady Margaret… is now Countess of Thanett, and is mother to ten children.'

Fortunately, Lady Anne's second daughter, Isabella, also survived.

Wet nurses

If the mother had died, was ill, or did not want to breastfeed her baby, it might be sent to a 'wet nurse' who would be able to breastfeed it for her. Often the wet nurse would have a baby of her own to feed.

Tudor children who were wet nursed and then 'placed out' with another family might spend only two or three years of their childhood living at home with their parents.

Wrapped up

New babies were wrapped in long strips of material known as 'swaddling bands' for the first few weeks. These pinned their arms to their sides and stopped them kicking their legs. People thought this made their arms and legs grow straight.

What's best or worst for baby

If no wet nurse could be found, the baby would be fed on 'pap', usually a mixture of water, milk and flour. This entry in the Earl of Northumberland's 1512 household accounts shows that babies and young children were fed with other unsuitable foods too:

'Breakfast for the Nurcery, for my Lady Margaret [aged three] and Mr Ingram Percy [aged one and a half] a manchet [a type of bread], one quart of beer, three mutton bones boiled.'

Victorian babies

Unlike Tudor mothers, wealthy Victorians could buy lots of things for their infants, including tinned baby food, which first appeared in the shops in 1867. Another great invention was the perambulator ('pram' for short) in the 1850s. It meant that babies did not have to be carried everywhere.

The first prams had no springs so babies would have had an uncomfortable ride

Early partings

Babies born in the nineteenth century had a better chance of survival than those born in the 1500s, but many still died.

When her son Herbert Almeric died in 1839, Mary Elizabeth Lucy of Charlecote Park in Warwickshire wrote:

'...so calm and sweet a parting it scarcely seemed like death... lovely as if asleep in that room that I call the fatal or death room, since every child born in it I have lived to mourn the death of'.

Did you know that in 1851 only 50 per cent of babies were expected to reach their fifth birthday?

Older children as well as babies were likely to die of diseases such as smallpox, typhoid or cholera. Diphtheria killed three of the Butcher children who lived at Wicken Fen in Cambridgeshire. The remains of Sarah, Harriet and George, who died aged nine, seven and four, lie in an unmarked grave in Wicken cemetery.

The children of rich Victorians were just as likely to succumb to disease – young Herbert Almeric Lucy was one of seven children, five of whom died during their mother's lifetime.

Don't wake the baby!

Poor Victorian mothers often had to work from home and needed to keep their infants quiet. Medicines were available from the chemist, with names like *Mrs Wilkinson's Soothing Syrup* and *Atkinson's Royal Infant's Preservative*, most of which contained the drug opium. Babies as young as one month old were given large doses of these medicines, and some died as a result.

Going to school in Tudor times

Noblemen's sons were taught at home by tutors, but most boys went to school. Grammar school boys were expected to attend school every day, but boys from poor families who went to parish schools often had to stay at home and help their fathers. Even so, most boys managed to learn enough to be able to write their name and to say the Lord's Prayer in Latin. It was different for girls, who received hardly any education.

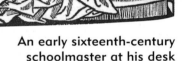

An early sixteenth-century schoolmaster at his desk

The long school day

Every day except Sunday, boys arrived at school very early in the morning and did not leave until 5 or 6 o'clock. Divinity (scripture) and Latin were the most important subjects, but arithmetic, Greek and music were also taught. With over 60 boys of all ages in one room and only two masters, there must have been plenty of opportunity to muck about.

Henry Percy, Earl of Northumberland, began a long letter of parental advice when his first son was born in 1595. He thought that Latin was most important:

'…*other languages are good and profitable, yet to be laid aside, until their own and Latin be perfected*'.

One fifteenth-century tutor complained that his pupils kept finding an excuse to leave the room:

'As sone as I am cum into the schole, this felow goeth to make water.'

Housewives in the making

Most girls received no formal education at all, although many could read, write, and do enough maths to keep the household accounts. Highly educated women such as Queen Elizabeth, who spoke nine languages, and her stepmother Catherine Parr, whose book *Prayers and Meditations* was published in 1545, were very unusual.

No spelling mistakes!

Tudor schoolboys wrote with quill pens which they dipped into pots of ink. They had to sharpen their quills every day with special knives which we still call 'penknives'.

They didn't have to worry about learning to spell, as there were no right or wrong spellings. Words were spelt however the writer thought they sounded. They could spell their names any way they wanted, as well.

> **Spell your own name in the Tudor way, as it sounds. Does it look very different?**

Career choices

Clever boys intending to enter the Church or study law, went to university at Oxford, Cambridge or the Inns of Court in London. Noblemen's sons who hoped to attend the royal court needed also to learn how to joust, play tennis, sing, dance and play musical instruments, as well as be good horsemen.

Tudor handwriting: an example in the Latin exercise book of Edward VI

> **Tudor girls spent their time helping the women with their work. They learnt spinning and sewing, making candles and soap, growing vegetables, and cooking – skills like these were known as 'housewifery'.**

Lord Northumberland, like most Tudors, did not think that education was important for girls. Their role in life was to:

'…bring up their children well into their long coat age, to tend their healths and education, to obey their husbands…'

Charm school

Girls who were going to attend court were supposed to be graceful and charming. Music was an important part of their education, learning to dance and sing, and perhaps to play the lute, the virginals (a keyboard instrument) or the harp.

Going to school in Victorian times

Boys from wealthier Victorian families went to the grammar schools that had been founded for their Tudor ancestors over 300 years before. The sons of rich parents were sent away to public schools, where they boarded during term-time. Schools such as Eton, Harrow and Rugby aimed to give boys a 'gentleman's education'. Good sportsmanship and being generally 'decent' were thought to be more important than having the best marks. But most children in the 1830s did not attend school at all.

'Keep them at home'

The ideal place for women was thought to be in the home, so girls from rich families were educated at home, usually by a governess.

The position of governess was a lonely one. They were seen as being 'above' the servants but 'below' the family, and were unable to mix with either. Charlotte Brönte, author of *Jane Eyre*, was a governess for a time. She remembered how one of her pupils told her that he loved her. His mother, overhearing, said, 'Love the *governess*, dear?' as if such a thing was impossible.

This is how wealthy Ada and Linda Fairfax-Lucy spent their day at Charlecote Park in Warwickshire, in the 1870s:

'Prayers before breakfast, harp and piano practice in the morning, drives in the pony carriage with mother in the afternoon..., reading and studying before tea, music in the library after dinner, then more prayers before bedtime.'

Children from the Wyndham family with their governess at Petworth, West Sussex

Education for all?

Neither boys nor girls from most ordinary families had very much education.

Government rulings about schools were only introduced in 1870, with the Education Act. This said that all children had to attend school until they were ten; as a result special primary schools were set up and pupils took along a few pence each week, to pay for their education.

Girls who were supposed to attend these schools were often kept back to look after the house or mind the baby. By the end of the century, they were receiving lessons in cooking, housework, and laundry.

Put it on the slate

Young children wrote on a mini blackboard called a slate, using a slate pencil which could be rubbed out afterwards.

Older children used inkpens on paper. Unlike Tudor children, Victorians had to work hard at spelling. They also had to spend hours copying out poems and essays to improve their handwriting.

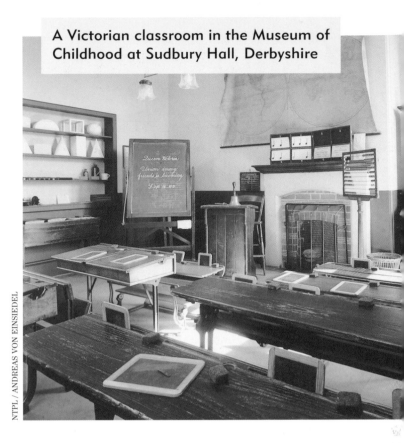

A Victorian classroom in the Museum of Childhood at Sudbury Hall, Derbyshire

NTPL / ANDREAS VON EINSIEDEL

Opportunities for girls

One of the first schools for girls from wealthy families was Cheltenham Ladies College, opened in 1853. Its pupils studied Greek, Latin and literature. Not many parents wanted to send their daughters there at first. One of the principals, Dorothea Beale, explained that this was because the name 'college' frightened people:

'...it was said that girls would be turned into boys, if they attended a college'.

Universities were very slow in opening their doors to young women. London University admitted women in 1848, but there were no women's colleges in Oxford or Cambridge until the 1870s. Even then, female students were not permitted to collect their degrees, although they often got better marks than the men.

Clothes for Tudor children

Until the age of four or five, boys and girls wore the same clothes, long skirts and aprons. After this, boys were 'breeched', dressed in their first set of men's clothes: a shirt, a doublet (jacket), and a pair of hose (tights). Girls wore miniature versions of women's chemises, bodices and skirts – there were no special clothes for children.

Arabella Stuart aged fourteen

Knowing your place

The Tudors thought that clothes showed how important someone was. Ordinary people were not allowed to wear anything made from expensive material or coloured red or purple. If they did, they could be fined! Rich people wore stiff, impractical clothes, which showed that they had no need to work.

Pudding bands

After swaddling for four to six weeks, babies were put into loose frocks. As they began to learn to walk, pieces of padded cloth called 'pudding bands' were wrapped round their heads to protect them when they fell over.

A portrait of the Lucy children, 1619: three girls and their baby brother all wear bodices and skirts

Lady Anne Clifford, living at Knole in Kent, made a note in her diary when her daughter Margaret was three years old:

'I cut the child's strings [leading reins] from her coats... she had 2 or 3 falls but had no hurt with them.'

Clothes for Victorian children

At the start of the nineteenth century children still wore small versions of adults' clothes. The custom of 'breeching' continued but most Victorian boys put on male clothes earlier, at the age of two or three. Boys from poor families often went on wearing their big sisters' hand-me-downs because they had no trousers. Boys wore knickerbockers (short trousers) with a shirt and jacket until they graduated to long trousers in their teens.

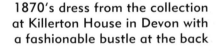

1870's dress from the collection at Killerton House in Devon with a fashionable bustle at the back

Stiff, starchy, tight and itchy

The girls especially had an uncomfortable time: they might have to wear crinolines and laced-up corsets to pull in their waists as tightly as possible, which was the Victorian fashion.

By the 1880s, however, children's clothes were becoming less fussy, with softer materials and looser shapes, so children could run around and play more easily.

Girls still had to wear large, heavy hats, and boys still wore stiff, high collars. Both sexes had woollen stockings and underwear, which must have been very itchy.

Snug as a bug

Victorian babies were lucky because they didn't have to wear swaddling bands. They wore long flannel petticoats and heavy towelling nappies with ties to keep them in place.

When someone in the family died, there was a period of mourning when girls and women had to wear special clothes. 'Deepest mourning' meant wearing only black. Then it might be grey or mauve. Men and boys wore black arm-bands and ties.

Mourning usually lasted three years but when Prince Albert died in 1861, Queen Victoria stayed in mourning for the rest of her life – 40 years!

25

Tudor children at work

The commonest job for a man in Tudor England was farm work, and boys learnt the skills of husbandry by working alongside their fathers. Girls usually learnt housewifery by helping their mothers at home or in the vegetable garden.

From the time they could walk, boys were put to work in the fields. They scared birds away from the crops and picked up stones to make the earth easier to plough.

When they were older, boys often looked after their family's sheep and cows which grazed on the 'common land' of the village, land which everyone could use.

Servant life

Some children had jobs in domestic service. Country boys sometimes became servants in the houses of wealthy Tudor landowners (see page 15). They trained as gardeners, stewards, serving men or cooks. Boys started off as unpaid apprentices and learnt new skills on the job. Most cooks started as kitchen boys, fetching wood for the fire, turning the roasting spit and washing the dishes.

A kitchen boy would turn the meat as it cooked on the spit in this roasting hearth at Cotehele, Cornwall

NTPL / ANDREAS VON EINSIEDEL

Apprentice boys

Most of the children who worked in Tudor towns were apprentices. Being an apprentice was thought to be a good way for a boy to learn a trade. It usually took seven years, and boys could train for a whole range of jobs from blacksmith, tailor, mason (builder) to printer, glass-maker, clock-maker, or armourer (maker of armour and weapons).

Pickpockets

There were many poor or orphaned children who lived on the streets of the towns. To survive they had to beg, steal food or pick people's pockets. This was called 'cutting purses'. Clothes did not have pockets at this time and people usually carried their money in little bags called purses, which they tied to their belts.

In 1585, an alehouse (pub) keeper called Wotton was charged with keeping 'a schole house sett up to learne [teach] yonge boys to cutt purses'.

Begging for charity

At this time, people with no job or money did not get help from the state, so there was a real chance of starving or freezing to death. Many rich people felt that part of their Christian duty was to give charity to the poor in the form of money, food or medicine, but what they gave was not enough to look after everybody.

Several laws were passed to try and help poor children. In 1536, every parish was required to collect beggars aged five to fourteen and give them apprenticeships in unskilled jobs.

The Poor Relief Act of 1598 made parishes responsible for feeding and clothing poor orphans. This law remained in force until 1834 – only three years before the start of Queen Victoria's reign.

Victorian children at work

One result of the Industrial Revolution was that many families left the countryside to look for work in the towns. As soon as the children were old enough (sometimes as early as six or seven), they were sent out to work in the factories.

Nodding off

Children working ten hours a day had no time for school, so they were sometimes given lessons in the evenings. The trouble was that they were often so tired they fell asleep at their books, or under dangerous factory machinery. Eventually, laws were passed to shorten their working day.

Below stairs

In the 1870s one third of all British girls between the ages of twelve and twenty went 'into service', which meant that they became housemaids or kitchen maids. This was not an easy life, as the wages were low and they had little time to themselves.

Some employers were strict. Mrs Smith, housekeeper in the 1860s at Petworth House, West Sussex, made sure that:

'...no maid was allowed to go into the town, their dress was most severely regulated... attendance at church was strictly enforced...'

Lower servants, such as kitchen maids, were not allowed into the family rooms of grand houses, such as the drawing room or library. At Wallington, a house in Northumberland, they were expected to avoid meeting the family or their guests on the stairs or in the passages. Servants could be sacked very easily.

Hard labour

Quarry Bank Mill is a cotton mill at Styal in Cheshire, which employed 90 'pauper apprentices' until 1847. The children were either orphans, or they were 'given' to the mill by parents who could not afford to feed and clothe them. They worked twelve hours a day, six days a week, in return for food, a shared bed and a basic education.

Children slept two in a bed at Styal Apprentice House

NTPL / KEITH HEWITT

Kid gangs

In the country, many labourers' children became 'gang workers'. These were gangs of children and adults who worked under a 'gang master' picking farmers' fruit and vegetables for very low wages. Some of the children were as young as six. One father described the work:

'My girl went 5 miles yesterday, to get to her work, turniping, she set off between 7 and 8, she walked, had a piece of bread before she went, she did not stop work in the middle of the day, ate nothing until she left off, she came home between 3 and 4 o'clock.'

The Education Act of 1876 finally made it illegal to employ children under ten in agricultural work.

The poorest of the poor

London was full of street children, orphaned or abandoned. Some managed to scrape a living as crossing-sweepers, who made sure that fine ladies and gentlemen did not get mud and horse manure on their shoes when they crossed the road.

Other poor children became 'mudlarks' who searched in the mud of riverbanks for any object they could sell for a few pennies.

The Tudor idea of fun

On the whole, Tudor parents thought that playing was a waste of time. They wanted their children to be at school or working. However, children did manage to find some time to enjoy themselves. On their way to Durham School, the boys were always 'bursting glassen windows, overthrowing milkmaid's pailes, pulling down stalles'.

Football hooligans

During the Tudor period there were no organised games such as cricket or hockey for children to play. Boys might join the men in playing a type of soccer, using a blown-up pig's bladder as a ball. There were no rules, and the game was played over a large area, sometimes with the two goal posts in different villages. It's not surprising that people were often hurt during these games.

Tudor toys

There were hoops, dolls, drums and hobby-horses, usually made at home, out of wood. Very few of these toys survive, but they can sometimes be seen in paintings of Tudor children.

> *I am called childhood, in play is all my mind,*
> *To cast a quoit, a cockshy, and a ball.*
> *A top can I set, and drive it in his kind...*

Four Tudor toys are mentioned in a poem by Sir Thomas More, Henry VIII's Lord Chancellor

Fairy tales

Tudor children did not have any books written specially for them except instruction manuals about polite behaviour. According to the *Boke of Nurture*, written in the mid-sixteenth century, reading 'fayried fables' would bring 'much mischief' to children.

The Victorian idea of fun

Wealthy children grew up in nurseries full of toys and books. Some were educational or religious, such as the ABC and Noah's Ark. Others were preparations for adult life – boys played with tin soldiers and girls played with doll's houses.

Sport for fun

Games were an organised business. Wealthy boys played cricket and rugby, most boys played football. These games had nearly all the rules that they have today. By the end of the Victorian era, girls were playing tennis, skating and riding bicycles, like boys.

Victorian toys were often made for rich children by poor children.

A picture called *Toy Makers and Toy Breakers* shows a bare room with ragged children making toys by candlelight, and a group of rich children in a luxurious nursery.

NTPL / ANDREAS VON EINSIEDEL

This doll's house, made in the 1880s, is now at Wallington: it has 36 rooms, electric light, a lift, running water and 77 dolls to live in it!

Victorians loved to collect all sorts of things. Philately (stamp collecting) began with the first stamps issued in the 1840s; other favoured objects were bird's eggs and butterflies.

Rosalie Chichester, who lived at Arlington Court in Devon, collected shells and model ships throughout her life.

Children's classics

People spent a lot of their spare time reading. Public libraries were set up so that those who could not afford to buy books would be able to read too. Many famous children's books, including *Alice's Adventures in Wonderland*, *Black Beauty* and *Treasure Island*, were written in the Victorian era.

Toy collections to see:

- Arlington Court, Devon
- Sudbury Hall Museum of Childhood and Calke Abbey in Derbyshire
- Ickworth, Suffolk
- Nostell Priory and Nunnington Hall in Yorkshire
- Townend, Cumbria
- Wallington, Northumberland

Places to visit

Visit these properties
and find out more about
life during Tudor and
Victorian times:

Tudor

**Little Moreton Hall,
Cheshire:** a dramatic, half-
timbered house *(below)*.

NTPL / RUPERT TRUMAN

Sutton House, Hackney:
built by one of Henry VIII's
courtiers in 1535.

**Charlecote Park,
Warwickshire:** a brick house
with great twisted chimneys,
set in a deer park and
visited by Elizabeth I.

The National Curriculum

*Investigating Childhood in
Tudor and Victorian Times*
provides useful background
information for children
covering history topics
at **Key Stage 2**.

**Montacute House,
Somerset:** built by a
successful Elizabethan
lawyer, it now houses
Tudor paintings from the
National Portrait Gallery.

Hardwick Hall, Derbyshire:
built by Bess of Hardwick,
one of England's very finest
sixteenth-century houses.

**Marker's Cottage, Killerton,
Devon:** see how most people
lived in Tudor times, at this
cottage made of cob (a mix
of clay and straw).

Victorian

Cragside, Northumberland:
a rambling mansion with
landscaped estate and
gardens, built for a wealthy
Victorian industrialist.

**Penrhyn Castle, North
Wales:** looks like a Norman
castle, but was built in the
nineteenth century as a
country house.

Carlyle's House, Chelsea:
London home of the writer,
Thomas Carlyle.

Lanhydrock, Cornwall: a
country house rebuilt in the
1880s and hardly changed
since, with fine kitchens,
nurseries and attics.

Standen, West Sussex: a
family house built in the
1890s, with furnishings in
the latest style of the time,
known as Arts and Crafts.

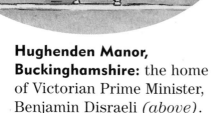

**Hughenden Manor,
Buckinghamshire:** the home
of Victorian Prime Minister,
Benjamin Disraeli *(above)*.

For a full list of National
Trust properties, see *The
National Trust Handbook*,
available from National Trust
shops and good bookshops.

FRONT COVER PICTURES
A scene from Tudor times in
the gallery at Little Moreton
Hall; A Victorian street at
Styal, Cheshire.

BACK COVER PICTURES
Young Arabella Stuart, at
Hardwick Hall (NTPL / JOHN
HAMMOND); Rocking horse at
Berrington Hall, Herefordshire
(NTPL / NADIA MACKENZIE).

First published in 2001 by
National Trust (Enterprises) Ltd,
36 Queen Anne's Gate,
London SW1H 9AS

Registered Charity No. 205846

© The National Trust 2001

ISBN 0 7078 0335 7

Designed by Gill Mouqué

Printed and bound by Wing King
Tong Ltd, Hong Kong/China